HAL•LEONARD

BLUES
PLAY-ALONG

k & CD for B♭, E♭, Bass Clef and C instruments

VOLUME 13

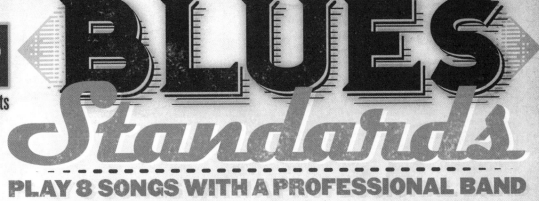

BLUES
Standards
PLAY 8 SONGS WITH A PROFESSIONAL BAND

D0504039

HOW TO USE THE CD:

Each song has <u>two</u> tracks:

1) Full Stereo Mix

All recorded instruments are present on this track.

2) Split Track

Piano and **Bass** parts can be removed
by turning down the volume on the LEFT channel.

Guitar parts can be removed
by turning down the volume on the RIGHT channel.

ISBN 978-1-4234-9648-9

HAL•LEONARD®
CORPORATION

7777 W. BLUEMOUND RD. P.O. BOX 13819 MILWAUKEE, WI 53213

Visit Hal Leonard Online at
www.halleonard.com

BOOK

CD

AIN'T NOBODY'S BUSINESS

WORDS AND MUSIC BY CLARENCE WILLIAMS, JAMES WITHERSPOON, PORTER GRAINGER AND ROBERT PRINCE

ADDITIONAL LYRICS

2. ME AND MY BABE, OH, WE FUSS AND FIGHT
   AND THEN THE NEXT MINUTE, EVERYTHING IS ALRIGHT,
   AND IT AIN'T NOBODY'S BUSINESS WHAT WE DO.

3. ONE DAY I THINK I'M GOING CRAZY,
   AND THE NEXT DAY I'M LAID BACK AND LAZY,
   AND IT AIN'T NOBODY'S BUSINESS IF I DO.

4. ONE DAY, I MIGHT TAKE A NOTION
   TO GO RIGHT DOWN AND JUMP IN THE OCEAN.
   AND IT AIN'T NOBODY'S BUSINESS IF I DO.

Kansas City

Words and Music by Jerry Leiber and Mike Stoller

ADDITIONAL LYRICS

2. I'LL BE STANDIN' ON THE CORNER OF TWELFTH STREET AND VINE.
I'LL BE STANDIN' ON THE CORNER OF TWELFTH STREET AND VINE.
WITH MY KANSAS CITY WOMAN AND A BOTTLE OF KANSAS CITY WINE.

Key to the Highway

Words and Music by Big Bill Broonzy and Chas. Segar

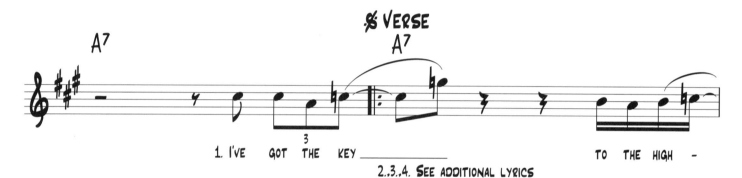

GUITAR/KEYS SOLOS

⊕ CODA OUTRO SOLO

ADDITIONAL LYRICS

2. I'm going back to the border,
   Baby, where I'm better known.
   Because you haven't done nothing, baby,
   But drove a good man from home.

3. When the moon peeks o'er the mountain,
   Little girl, I'll be on my way.
   I'm gonna roam the highway
   Until the break of day.

4. Oh, give me one more kiss, darlin',
   Just before I go.
   'Cause when I leave this time, little girl,
   I won't be back no more.

Let the Good Times Roll

Words and Music by Sam Theard and Fleecie Moore

Intro
Moderate Blues ♩ = 111

Verse

1. Hey, ev-'ry-bod-y, let's have some fun. You on-ly live but once, _ and when you're
2.,3. See additional lyrics

dead you're done. _ Let the good time roll, _____ let the

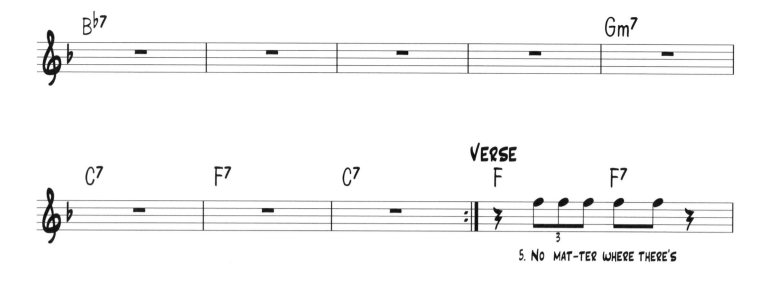

5. No mat-ter where there's

RAIN - Y WEATH - ER   BIRDS OF A FEATH-ER GOT TO STICK TO-GETH-ER.

SO   GET YOUR-SELF UN - DER CON - TROL,   GO OUT AND GET TO-

GETH-ER   AND LET THE GOOD TIMES ROLL.

ADDITIONAL LYRICS

2. DON'T SIT THERE A MUMBLIN', AND TALKIN' TRASH.
IF YOU WANNA HAVE A BALL YOU GOTTA SPEND SOME CASH.
LET THE GOOD TIMES ROLL, LET THE GOOD TIMES ROLL.
DON'T CARE IF YOU'RE YOUNG OR OLD,
GET TOGETHER, LET THE GOOD TIMES ROLL.

3. HEY, MR. LANDLORD, LOCK UP ALL THE DOORS.
WHEN THE POLICE COME AROUND, JUST TELL 'EM THE JOINT IS CLOSED.
LET THE GOOD TIMES ROLL, LET THE GOOD TIMES ROLL.
DON'T CARE IF YOU'RE YOUNG OR OLD,
GET TOGETHER, LET THE GOOD TIMES ROLL.

See See Rider

Words and Music by Ma Rainey

Additional Lyrics

2. Gonna buy me a pistol just as long as I am tall.
   Gonna buy me a pistol just as long as I am tall.
   I'm gonna shoot that man and catch a cannon ball.

3. See See Rider, where did you stay last night?
   See See Rider, where did you stay last night?
   Your shoes ain't laced, your clothes ain't fittin' you right.

Night Time is the Right Time

Words and Music by Roosevelt Sykes and James Oden

INTRO
MODERATE BLUES ♩. = 81

1. You know the night-time, dar-lin', is the
2., 3. See additional lyrics

right time to be _____ with the one you

love, now. Say now, oh, ba - by, well now, come on, ba -

by, now, I wan-na be the one you love, now. You the one I'm think-in'

of. And the night - time is the right

KEYS/GUITAR SOLOS

2. YOU KNOW MY

ADDITIONAL LYRICS

2. YOU KNOW MY MOTHER, NOW, HADN'T DIED NOW,
AND MY FATHER LEFT ME POOR CHILD CRYIN'.
SAY NOW, OH, BABY, WELL NOW, COME ON, BABY, NOW,
I WANT YOU TO HOLD MY HAND.
YEAH, TIGHT AS YOU CAN.
AND THE NIGHT TIME IS THE RIGHT TIME
TO BE WITH THE ONE YOU LOVE.

3. I SAID BABY, BABY, BABY, OH, BABY NOW.
OH, COME ON, BABY. YOU KNOW I WANT YOU BY MY SIDE.
WELL, I WANT YOU TO KEEP, OH, KEEP ME SATISFIED NOW.
I KNOW THAT NIGHT TIME, EVERY DAY IS THE RIGHT TIME
TO BE WITH THE ONE YOU LOVE.

Route 66

By Bobby Troup

INTRO
MODERATE SWING ♩ = 152

Verse

you _____ ev - er plan to mo - tor West ____
2. See additional lyrics

trav - el my way, take the high - way that's the best. ___

Get your kicks on Route ___ Six - ty - Six!

To Coda

1.
2. It

2.
3. Now you

GO through Saint Loo - ey and Jop - lin, Mis-sou - ri, and Ok - la - ho - ma Cit - y is might-

ADDITIONAL LYRICS

2. It winds from Chicago to L.A.
   More than two thousand miles all the way.
   Get your kicks on Route Sixty-Six!

4. Won't you get hip to this timely trip
   When you make that California trip.
   Get your kicks on Route Sixty-Six!

ADDITIONAL LYRICS

2. LIFE IS BARE, GLOOM AND MIS'RY EV'RYWHERE,
STORMY WEATHER, JUST CAN'T GET MY POOR SELF TOGETHER,
I'M WEARY ALL THE TIME, THE TIME,
SO WEARY ALL THE TIME.

Ain't Nobody's Business

Words and Music by Clarence Williams, James Witherspoon, Porter Grainger and Robert Prince

CD TRACK
1. Full Stereo Mix
9. Split Mix

B♭ Version

Additional Lyrics

2. Me and my babe, oh, we fuss and fight
   And then the next minute, everything is alright,
   And it ain't nobody's business what we do.

3. One day I think I'm going crazy,
   And the next day I'm laid back and lazy,
   And it ain't nobody's business if I do.

4. One day, I might take a notion
   To go right down and jump in the ocean.
   And it ain't nobody's business if I do.

Kansas City

Words and Music by Jerry Leiber and Mike Stoller

ADDITIONAL LYRICS

2. I'll be standin' on the corner of Twelfth Street and Vine.
   I'll be standin' on the corner of Twelfth Street and Vine.
   With my Kansas City woman and a bottle of Kansas City wine.

23

Key to the Highway
Words and Music by Big Bill Broonzy and Chas. Segar

1. I've got the key _____ to the high -

2..3..4. See additional lyrics

- way, _____ Billed out ____ and bound to go. ____

Gon - na leave ____ here run - nin'.

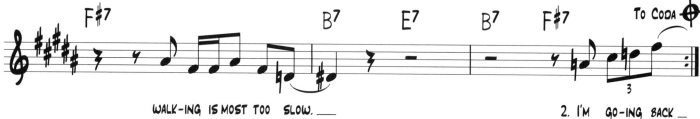

Walk-ing is most too slow. ____ 2. I'm go-ing back __

Guitar/Keys Solos

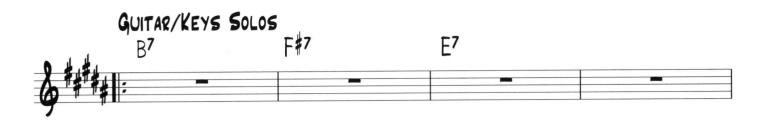

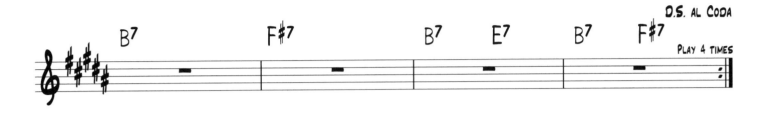

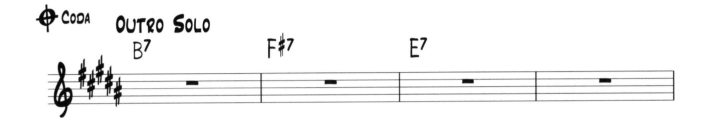

Coda **Outro Solo**

Additional Lyrics

2. I'm going back to the border,
   Baby, where I'm better known.
   Because you haven't done nothing, baby,
   But drove a good man from home.

3. When the moon peeks o'er the mountain,
   Little girl, I'll be on my way.
   I'm gonna roam the highway
   Until the break of day.

4. Oh, give me one more kiss, darlin',
   Just before I go.
   'Cause when I leave this time, little girl,
   I won't be back no more.

Let the Good Times Roll

Words and Music by Sam Theard and Fleecie Moore

Intro
Moderate Blues ♩ = 111

Verse

1. Hey, ev-'ry-bod-y, let's have some fun. You on-ly live but once, _ and when you're
2.,3. See additional lyrics

dead you're done. _ Let the good time roll, _____ let the

ADDITIONAL LYRICS

2. DON'T SIT THERE A MUMBLIN', AND TALKIN' TRASH.
   IF YOU WANNA HAVE A BALL YOU GOTTA SPEND SOME CASH.
   LET THE GOOD TIMES ROLL, LET THE GOOD TIMES ROLL.
   DON'T CARE IF YOU'RE YOUNG OR OLD.
   GET TOGETHER, LET THE GOOD TIMES ROLL.

3. HEY, MR. LANDLORD, LOCK UP ALL THE DOORS.
   WHEN THE POLICE COME AROUND, JUST TELL 'EM THE JOINT IS CLOSED.
   LET THE GOOD TIMES ROLL, LET THE GOOD TIMES ROLL.
   DON'T CARE IF YOU'RE YOUNG OR OLD.
   GET TOGETHER, LET THE GOOD TIMES ROLL.

See See Rider
Words and Music by Ma Rainey

Additional Lyrics

2. Gonna buy me a pistol just as long as I am tall.
Gonna buy me a pistol just as long as I am tall.
I'm gonna shoot that man and catch a cannon ball.

3. See See Rider, where did you stay last night?
See See Rider, where did you stay last night?
Your shoes ain't laced, your clothes ain't fittin' you right.

Night Time is the Right Time

Words and Music by Roosevelt Sykes and James Oden

1. You know the night-time, dar-lin', is the
2., 3. See additional lyrics

right time to be _____ with the one you love, now. Say now, oh, ba-by, well now, come on, ba-

by, now. I wan-na be the one you love, now. You the one I'm think-in'

of. And the night-time is the right

Keys/Guitar Solos

Additional Lyrics

2. You know my mother, now, hadn't died now,
   And my father left me poor child cryin'.
   Say now, oh, baby, well now, come on, baby, now,
   I want you to hold my hand.
   Yeah, tight as you can.
   And the night time is the right time
   To be with the one you love.

3. I said baby, baby, baby, oh, baby now.
   Oh, come on, baby. You know I want you by my side.
   Well, I want you to keep, oh, keep me satisfied now.
   I know that night time, every day is the right time
   To be with the one you love.

ROUTE 66
BY BOBBY TROUP

INTRO
MODERATE SWING ♩ = 152

N.C.

E13

1. If

Verse

A7 ... D7 ... A7

YOU _____ EV - ER PLAN TO MO - TOR WEST _____
2. See additional lyrics

D7

TRAV - EL MY WAY, TAKE THE HIGH - WAY THAT'S THE BEST. _

A7 ... Bm7 ... E7

GET YOUR KICKS ON ROUTE _ SIX - TY - SIX! _

A7 ... To Coda ⊕ 1. ... E7 ... 2. E7

_____ 2. IT ... 3. NOW YOU

A7 N.C. ... Eb9 ... D9 N.C. ... Bb7 ... A7 N.C.

GO THROUGH SAINT LOO - EY AND JOP - LIN, MIS-SOU - RI, AND OK - LA - HO - MA CIT - Y IS MIGHT-

STORMY WEATHER
(KEEPS RAININ' ALL THE TIME)
LYRIC BY TED KOEHLER
MUSIC BY HAROLD ARLEN

Additional Lyrics

2. Life is bare, gloom and mis'ry ev'rywhere,
   Stormy weather. Just can't get my poor self together.
   I'm weary all the time, the time,
   So weary all the time.

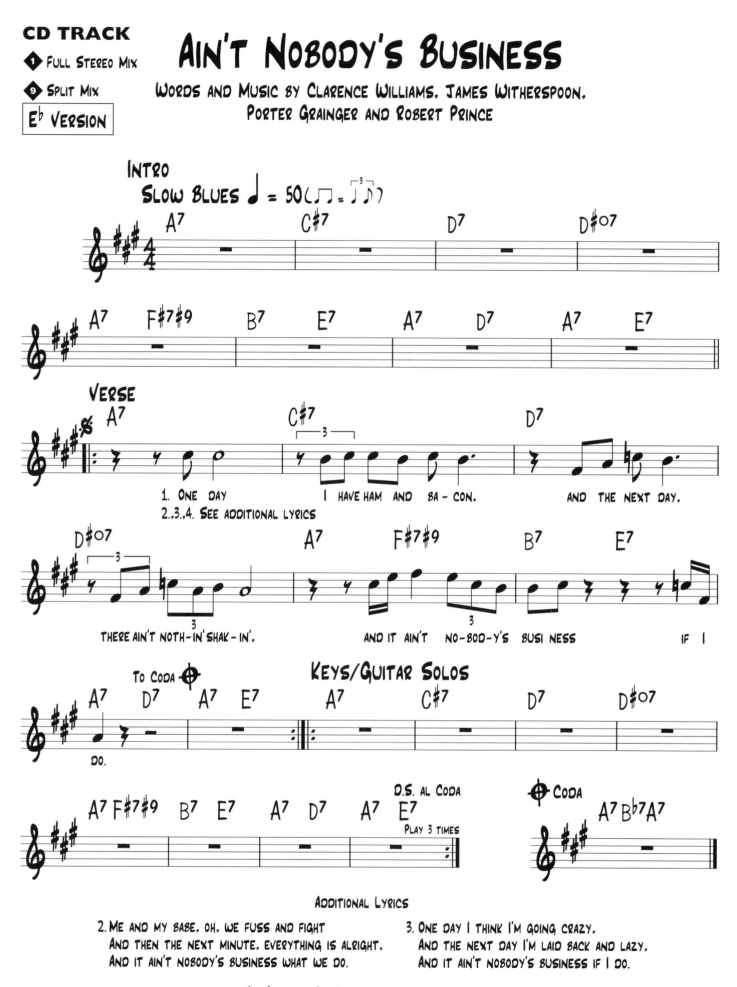

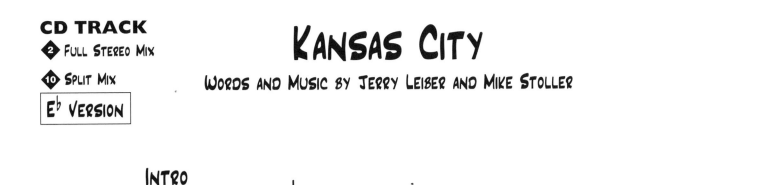

Kansas City

Words and Music by Jerry Leiber and Mike Stoller

GUITAR/KEYS SOLOS

ADDITIONAL LYRICS

2. I'll be standin' on the corner of Twelfth Street and Vine.
I'll be standin' on the corner of Twelfth Street and Vine.
With my Kansas City woman and a bottle of Kansas City wine.

Key to the Highway

Words and Music by Big Bill Broonzy and Chas. Segar

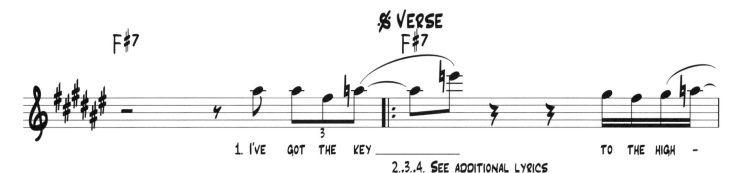

1. I've got the key ___ to the high-

2., 3., 4. See additional lyrics

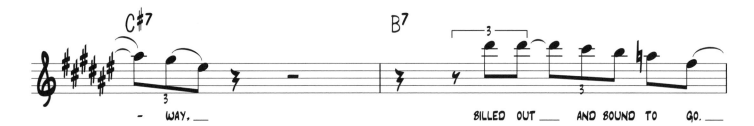

- way, ___ Billed out ___ and bound to go.

___ Gon-na leave ___ here run-nin'.

Walk-ing is most too slow. ___ 2. I'm go-ing back ___

Guitar/Keys Solos

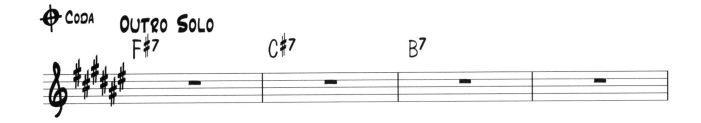

Additional Lyrics

2. I'm going back to the border,
   Baby, where I'm better known.
   Because you haven't done nothing, baby,
   But drove a good man from home.

3. When the moon peeks o'er the mountain,
   Little girl, I'll be on my way.
   I'm gonna roam the highway
   Until the break of day.

4. Oh, give me one more kiss, darlin',
   Just before I go.
   'Cause when I leave this time, little girl,
   I won't be back no more.

Let the Good Times Roll

Words and Music by Sam Theard and Fleecie Moore

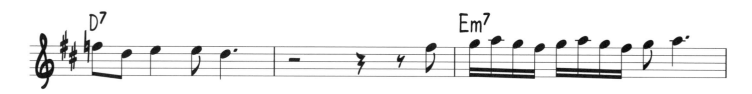

1. Hey, ev-'ry-bod-y,   let's have some fun.   You   on-ly live but once, __ and when you're

2..3. See additional lyrics

dead you're done. __ Let the good time roll. _____   Let the

Additional Lyrics

2. Don't sit there a mumblin', and talkin' trash.
   If you wanna have a ball you gotta spend some cash.
   Let the good times roll. Let the good times roll.
   Don't care if you're young or old.
   Get together, let the good times roll.

3. Hey, Mr. Landlord, lock up all the doors.
   When the police come around, just tell 'em the joint is closed.
   Let the good times roll. Let the good times roll.
   Don't care if you're young or old.
   Get together, let the good times roll.

See See Rider
Words and Music by Ma Rainey

Additional Lyrics

2. Gonna buy me a pistol just as long as I am tall.
Gonna buy me a pistol just as long as I am tall.
I'm gonna shoot that man and catch a cannon ball.

3. See See Rider, where did you stay last night?
See See Rider, where did you stay last night?
Your shoes ain't laced, your clothes ain't fittin' you right.

Night Time
is the Right Time

Words and Music by Roosevelt Sykes and James Oden

Keys/Guitar Solos

Additional Lyrics

2. You know my mother, now, hadn't died now,
   And my father left me poor child cryin'.
   Say now, oh, baby, well now, come on, baby, now,
   I want you to hold my hand.
   Yeah, tight as you can.
   And the night time is the right time
   To be with the one you love.

3. I said baby, baby, baby, oh, baby now.
   Oh, come on, baby. You know I want you by my side.
   Well, I want you to keep, oh, keep me satisfied now.
   I know that night time, every day is the right time
   To be with the one you love.

CD TRACK

◆ 6 Full Stereo Mix

◆ 14 Split Mix

E♭ Version

Route 66

By Bobby Troup

Intro
Moderate Swing ♩ = 152

N.C.

B13

1. If

% Verse

E7   A7   E7

you _____ ev - er plan to mo - tor west _____

2. See additional lyrics

A7

trav - el my way, take the high - way that's the best. _

E7   F#m7   B7

Get your kicks on Route _ six - ty - six! _

E7   To Coda ⊕ 1.   B7   2.   B7

_____   2. It   3. Now you

E7 N.C. B♭9 A9 N.C. F7 E7 N.C.

go through Saint Loo - ey and Jop - lin, Mis-sou-ri, and Ok-la-ho-ma Cit-y is might-

Guitar/Keys Solos

D.S. al Coda
Play 4 times

Coda

Additional Lyrics

2. It winds from Chicago to L.A.
   More than two thousand miles all the way.
   Get your kicks on Route Sixty-Six!

4. Won't you get hip to this timely trip
   When you make that California trip.
   Get your kicks on Route Sixty-Six!

Additional Lyrics

2. Life is bare, gloom and mis'ry ev'rywhere,
   Stormy weather, just can't get my poor self together,
   I'm weary all the time, the time,
   So weary all the time.

Ain't Nobody's Business

Words and Music by Clarence Williams, James Witherspoon, Porter Grainger and Robert Prince

1. One day I have ham and ba-con, and the next day, there ain't noth-in' shak-in', and it ain't no-bod-y's busi-ness if I do.

2.,3.,4. See additional lyrics

Additional Lyrics

2. Me and my babe, oh, we fuss and fight
   And then the next minute, everything is alright,
   And it ain't nobody's business what we do.

3. One day I think I'm going crazy,
   And the next day I'm laid back and lazy,
   And it ain't nobody's business if I do.

4. One day, I might take a notion
   To go right down and jump in the ocean.
   And it ain't nobody's business if I do.

Kansas City

Words and Music by Jerry Leiber and Mike Stoller

GUITAR/KEYS SOLOS

Additional Lyrics

2. I'll be standin' on the corner of Twelfth Street and Vine.
I'll be standin' on the corner of Twelfth Street and Vine.
With my Kansas City woman and a bottle of Kansas City wine.

Key to the Highway
Words and Music by Big Bill Broonzy and Chas. Segar

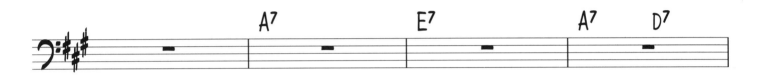

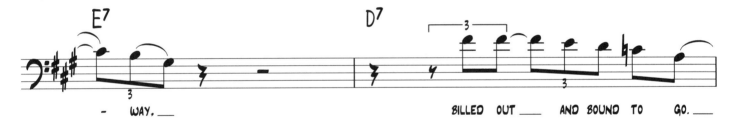

Guitar/Keys Solos

Coda

Outro Solo

Additional Lyrics

2. I'm going back to the border,
   Baby, where I'm better known.
   Because you haven't done nothing, baby,
   But drove a good man from home.

3. When the moon peeks o'er the mountain,
   Little girl, I'll be on my way.
   I'm gonna roam the highway
   Until the break of day.

4. Oh, give me one more kiss, darlin',
   Just before I go.
   'Cause when I leave this time, little girl,
   I won't be back no more.

Let the Good Times Roll

Words and Music by Sam Theard and Fleecie Moore

𝄢 C Version

1. Hey, ev-'ry-bod-y, let's have some fun. You on-ly live but once,__ and when you're
2.,3. See additional lyrics

dead you're done.__ Let the good time roll,_____ let the

Additional Lyrics

2. Don't sit there a mumblin', and talkin' trash.
If you wanna have a ball you gotta spend some cash.
Let the good times roll. Let the good times roll.
Don't care if you're young or old.
Get together, let the good times roll.

3. Hey, Mr. Landlord, lock up all the doors.
When the police come around, just tell 'em the joint is closed.
Let the good times roll. Let the good times roll.
Don't care if you're young or old.
Get together, let the good times roll.

See See Rider

Words and Music by Ma Rainey

Additional Lyrics

2. Gonna buy me a pistol just as long as I am tall.
Gonna buy me a pistol just as long as I am tall.
I'm gonna shoot that man and catch a cannon ball.

3. See See Rider, where did you stay last night?
See See Rider, where did you stay last night?
Your shoes ain't laced, your clothes ain't fittin' you right.

CD TRACK
5 Full Stereo Mix
13 Split Mix
🎼 C Version

Night Time is the Right Time

Words and Music by Roosevelt Sykes and James Oden

TIME TO BE WITH THE ONE YOU LOVE, NOW.

Keys/Guitar Solos

2. YOU KNOW MY

Additional Lyrics

2. YOU KNOW MY MOTHER, NOW, HADN'T DIED NOW,
   AND MY FATHER LEFT ME POOR CHILD CRYIN'.
   SAY NOW, OH, BABY, WELL NOW, COME ON, BABY, NOW,
   I WANT YOU TO HOLD MY HAND.
   YEAH, TIGHT AS YOU CAN.
   AND THE NIGHT TIME IS THE RIGHT TIME
   TO BE WITH THE ONE YOU LOVE.

3. I SAID BABY, BABY, BABY, OH, BABY NOW.
   OH, COME ON, BABY. YOU KNOW I WANT YOU BY MY SIDE.
   WELL, I WANT YOU TO KEEP, OH, KEEP ME SATISFIED NOW.
   I KNOW THAT NIGHT TIME, EVERY DAY IS THE RIGHT TIME
   TO BE WITH THE ONE YOU LOVE.

Route 66

By Bobby Troup

𝄢 C Version

Get your kicks on Route Sixty-Six!

Additional Lyrics

2. It winds from Chicago to L.A.
More than two thousand miles all the way.
Get your kicks on Route Sixty-Six!

4. Won't you get hip to this timely trip
When you make that California trip.
Get your kicks on Route Sixty-Six!

STORMY WEATHER
(KEEPS RAININ' ALL THE TIME)

LYRIC BY TED KOEHLER
MUSIC BY HAROLD ARLEN

CD TRACK
8 FULL STEREO MIX
16 SPLIT MIX
C VERSION

INTRO
SLOW BLUES ♩ = 60

Bb   G7b9   Cm7   F7   Bb   Bo7

VERSE

Cm7   F7   Bb   Bo7   Cm7   F7

1. DON'T KNOW WHY ___ THERE'S NO SUN UP IN THE SKY, STORM-Y
2. SEE ADDITIONAL LYRICS

Bb   Bb7   Eb   Ebm   Bb   G7b9

WEATH-ER. ___ SINCE MY MAN AND I AIN'T TO-GETH-ER. ___

C7b9   F7b9   Dm7   G7b9   Cm7   F7

KEEPS RAIN-IN' ALL ___ THE TIME. ___   2. LIFE IS

Bb   Eb   Bb   C7b9   F7b9

TIME, ___ THE TIME, ___ SO WEAR-Y ALL ___ THE

BRIDGE

Bb   Eb   Ebm   Bb

TIME. ___   WHEN HE WENT A-WAY, ___ THE BLUES WALKED IN AND MET ME.

Eb   Ebm   Bb   Eb   Ebm

IF HE STAYS A-WAY, ___ OLD ROCK-IN' CHAIR WILL GET ME. ALL I DO IS PRAY ___ THE LORD A-

HAL•LEONARD

BLUES PLAY-ALONG

For use with all the C, B♭, Bass Clef and E♭ Instruments, the Hal Leonard Blues Play-Along Series is the ultimate jamming tool for all blues musicians.

With easy-to-read lead sheets, and other split-track choices on the included CD, these first-of-a-kind packages will bring your local blues jam right into your house! Each song on the CD includes two tracks: a full stereo mix, and a split track mix with removable guitar, bass, piano, and harp parts. The CD is playable on any CD player, and is also enhanced so Mac and PC users can adjust the recording to any tempo without changing the pitch!

1. Chicago Blues
All Your Love (I Miss Loving) • Easy Baby • I Ain't Got You • I'm Your Hoochie Coochie Man • Killing Floor • Mary Had a Little Lamb • Messin' with the Kid • Sweet Home Chicago.
00843106 Book/CD Pack $12.99

2. Texas Blues
Hide Away • If You Love Me Like You Say • Mojo Hand • Okie Dokie Stomp • Pride and Joy • Reconsider Baby • T-Bone Shuffle • The Things That I Used to Do.
00843107 Book/CD Pack $12.99

3. Slow Blues
Don't Throw Your Love on Me So Strong • Five Long Years • I Can't Quit You Baby • I Just Want to Make Love to You • The Sky Is Crying • (They Call It) Stormy Monday (Stormy Monday Blues) • Sweet Little Angel • Texas Flood.
00843108 Book/CD Pack $12.99

4. Shuffle Blues
Beautician Blues • Bright Lights, Big City • Further on up the Road • I'm Tore Down • Juke • Let Me Love You Baby • Look at Little Sister • Rock Me Baby.
00843171 Book/CD Pack $12.99

5. B.B. King
Everyday I Have the Blues • It's My Own Fault Darlin' • Just Like a Woman • Please Accept My Love • Sweet Sixteen • The Thrill Is Gone • Why I Sing the Blues • You Upset Me Baby.
00843172 Book/CD Pack $14.99

6. Jazz Blues
Birk's Works • Blues in the Closet • Cousin Mary • Freddie Freeloader • Now's the Time • Tenor Madness • Things Ain't What They Used to Be • Turnaround.
00843175 Book/CD Pack $12.99

7. Howlin' Wolf
Built for Comfort • Forty-Four • How Many More Years • Killing Floor • Moanin' at Midnight • Shake for Me • Sitting on Top of the World • Smokestack Lightning.
00843176 Book/CD Pack $12.99

8. Blues Classics
Baby, Please Don't Go • Boom Boom • Born Under a Bad Sign • Dust My Broom • How Long, How Long Blues • I Ain't Superstitious • It Hurts Me Too • My Babe.
00843177 Book/CD Pack $12.99

9. Albert Collins
Brick • Collins' Mix • Don't Lose Your Cool • Frost Bite • Frosty • I Ain't Drunk • Master Charge • Trash Talkin'.
00843178 Book/CD Pack $12.99

10. Uptempo Blues
Cross Road Blues (Crossroads) • Give Me Back My Wig • Got My Mo Jo Working • The House Is Rockin' • Paying the Cost to Be the Boss • Rollin' and Tumblin' • Turn on Your Love Light • You Can't Judge a Book by the Cover.
00843179 Book/CD Pack $12.99

11. Christmas Blues
Back Door Santa • Blue Christmas • Dig That Crazy Santa Claus • Merry Christmas, Baby • Please Come Home for Christmas • Santa Baby • Soulful Christmas.
00843203 Book/CD Pack $12.99

12. Jimmy Reed
Ain't That Lovin' You Baby • Baby, What You Want Me to Do • Big Boss Man • Bright Lights, Big City • Going to New York • Honest I Do • You Don't Have to Go • You Got Me Dizzy.
00843204 Book/CD Pack $12.99

FOR MORE INFORMATION, SEE YOUR LOCAL MUSIC DEALER, OR WRITE TO:

HAL•LEONARD® CORPORATION
7777 W. BLUEMOUND RD. P.O. BOX 13819 MILWAUKEE, WI 53213

www.halleonard.com

1111

The Best-Selling Jazz Book of All Time Is Now Legal!

The Real Books are the most popular jazz books of all time. Since the 1970s, musicians have trusted these volumes to get them through every gig, night after night. The problem is that the books were illegally produced and distributed, without any regard to copyright law, or royalties paid to the composers who created these musical masterpieces.

Hal Leonard is very proud to present the first legitimate and legal editions of these books ever produced. You won't even notice the difference, other than all the notorious errors being fixed: the covers and typeface look the same, the song lists are nearly identical, and the price for our edition is even cheaper than the originals!

Every conscientious musician will appreciate that these books are now produced accurately and ethically, benefitting the songwriters that we owe for some of the greatest tunes of all time!

VOLUME 1
00240221	C Edition	$35.00
00240224	B♭ Edition	$35.00
00240225	E♭ Edition	$35.00
00240226	Bass Clef Edition	$35.00
00240292	C Edition 6 x 9	$30.00
00240339	B♭ Edition 6 x 9	$30.00
00451087	C Edition on CD-ROM	$25.00
00240302	A-D CD Backing Tracks	$24.99
00240303	E-J CD Backing Tracks	$24.95
00240304	L-R CD Backing Tracks	$24.95
00240305	S-Z CD Backing Tracks	$24.99
00110604	Book/USB Flash Drive Backing Tracks Pack	$79.99
00110599	USB Flash Drive Only	$50.00

VOLUME 2
00240222	C Edition	$35.50
00240227	B♭ Edition	$35.00
00240228	E♭ Edition	$35.00
00240229	Bass Clef Edition	$35.00
00240293	C Edition 6 x 9	$27.95
00451088	C Edition on CD-ROM	$27.99
00240351	A-D CD Backing Tracks	$24.99
00240352	E-I CD Backing Tracks	$24.99
00240353	J-R CD Backing Tracks	$24.99
00240354	S-Z CD Backing Tracks	$24.99

VOLUME 3
00240233	C Edition	$35.00
00240284	B♭ Edition	$35.00
00240285	E♭ Edition	$35.00
00240286	Bass Clef Edition	$35.00
00240338	C Edition 6 x 9	$30.00
00451089	C Edition on CD-ROM	$29.99

VOLUME 4
00240296	C Edition	$35.00
00103348	B♭ Edition	$35.00
00103349	E♭ Edition	$35.00
00103350	Bass Clef Edition	$35.00

VOLUME 5
00240349	C Edition	$35.00

Also available:
00240264	The Real Blues Book	$34.99
00310910	The Real Bluegrass Book	$29.99
00240137	Miles Davis Real Book	$19.95
00240355	The Real Dixieland Book	$29.99
00240235	The Duke Ellington Real Book	$19.99
00240348	The Real Latin Book	$35.00
00240358	The Charlie Parker Real Book	$19.99
00240331	The Bud Powell Real Book	$19.99
00240313	The Real Rock Book	$35.00
00240323	The Real Rock Book – Vol. 2	$35.00
00240359	The Real Tab Book – Vol. 1	$32.50
00240317	The Real Worship Book	$29.99

THE REAL CHRISTMAS BOOK
00240306	C Edition	$27.50
00240345	B♭ Edition	$27.50
00240346	E♭ Edition	$27.50
00240347	Bass Clef Edition	$27.50
00240431	A-G CD Backing Tracks	$24.99
00240432	H-M CD Backing Tracks	$24.99
00240433	N-Y CD Backing Tracks	$24.99

THE REAL VOCAL BOOK
00240230	Volume 1 High Voice	$35.00
00240307	Volume 1 Low Voice	$35.00
00240231	Volume 2 High Voice	$35.00
00240308	Volume 2 Low Voice	$35.00
00240391	Volume 3 High Voice	$29.99
00240392	Volume 3 Low Voice	$35.00

THE REAL BOOK – STAFF PAPER
00240327	$9.95

HOW TO PLAY FROM A REAL BOOK
FOR ALL MUSICIANS
by Robert Rawlins
00312097	$17.50

Complete song lists online at www.halleonard.com
Prices, content, and availability subject to change without notice.

HAL•LEONARD® CORPORATION
7777 W. BLUEMOUND RD. P.O. BOX 13819 MILWAUKEE, WI 53213

0313

Presenting the Hal Leonard JAZZ PLAY-ALONG SERIES

For use with all B-flat, E-flat, Bass Clef and C instruments, the Jazz Play-Along® Series is the ultimate learning tool for all jazz musicians. With musician-friendly lead sheets, melody cues, and other split-track choices on the included CD, these first-of-a-kind packages help you master improvisation while playing some of the greatest tunes of all time. FOR STUDY, each tune includes a split track with: melody cue with proper style and inflection • professional rhythm tracks • choruses for soloing • removable bass part • removable piano part. FOR PERFORMANCE, each tune also has: an additional full stereo accompaniment track (no melody) • additional choruses for soloing.

1A. MAIDEN VOYAGE/ALL BLUES
00843158 .... $15.99

1. DUKE ELLINGTON
00841644 .... $16.95

2. MILES DAVIS
00841645 .... $16.95

3. THE BLUES
00841646 .... $16.99

4. JAZZ BALLADS
00841691 .... $16.99

5. BEST OF BEBOP
00841689 .... $16.95

6. JAZZ CLASSICS WITH EASY CHANGES
00841690 .... $16.99

7. ESSENTIAL JAZZ STANDARDS
00843000 .... $16.99

8. ANTONIO CARLOS JOBIM AND THE ART OF THE BOSSA NOVA
00843001 .... $16.95

9. DIZZY GILLESPIE
00843002 .... $16.99

10. DISNEY CLASSICS
00843003 .... $16.99

11. RODGERS AND HART FAVORITES
00843004 .... $16.99

12. ESSENTIAL JAZZ CLASSICS
00843005 .... $16.99

13. JOHN COLTRANE
00843006 .... $16.95

14. IRVING BERLIN
00843007 .... $15.99

15. RODGERS & HAMMERSTEIN
00843008 .... $15.99

16. COLE PORTER
00843009 .... $15.95

17. COUNT BASIE
00843010 .... $16.95

18. HAROLD ARLEN
00843011 .... $15.95

19. COOL JAZZ
00843012 .... $15.95

20. CHRISTMAS CAROLS
00843080 .... $14.95

21. RODGERS AND HART CLASSICS
00843014 .... $14.95

22. WAYNE SHORTER
00843015 .... $16.95

23. LATIN JAZZ
00843016 .... $16.95

24. EARLY JAZZ STANDARDS
00843017 .... $14.95

25. CHRISTMAS JAZZ
00843018 .... $16.95

26. CHARLIE PARKER
00843019 .... $16.95

27. GREAT JAZZ STANDARDS
00843020 .... $16.99

28. BIG BAND ERA
00843021 .... $15.99

29. LENNON AND MCCARTNEY
00843022 .... $16.95

30. BLUES' BEST
00843023 .... $15.99

31. JAZZ IN THREE
00843024 .... $15.99

32. BEST OF SWING
00843025 .... $15.99

33. SONNY ROLLINS
00843029 .... $15.95

34. ALL TIME STANDARDS
00843030 .... $15.99

35. BLUESY JAZZ
00843031 .... $16.99

36. HORACE SILVER
00843032 .... $16.99

37. BILL EVANS
00843033 .... $16.95

38. YULETIDE JAZZ
00843034 .... $16.95

39. "ALL THE THINGS YOU ARE" & MORE JEROME KERN SONGS
00843035 .... $15.99

40. BOSSA NOVA
00843036 .... $16.99

41. CLASSIC DUKE ELLINGTON
00843037 .... $16.99

42. GERRY MULLIGAN FAVORITES
00843038 .... $16.99

43. GERRY MULLIGAN CLASSICS
00843039 .... $16.99

44. OLIVER NELSON
00843040 .... $16.95

45. GEORGE GERSHWIN
00103643 .... $24.99

46. BROADWAY JAZZ STANDARDS
00843042 .... $15.99

47. CLASSIC JAZZ BALLADS
00843043 .... $15.99

48. BEBOP CLASSICS
00843044 .... $16.99

49. MILES DAVIS STANDARDS
00843045 .... $16.95

50. GREAT JAZZ CLASSICS
00843046 .... $15.99

51. UP-TEMPO JAZZ
00843047 .... $15.99

52. STEVIE WONDER
00843048 .... $16.99

53. RHYTHM CHANGES
00843049 .... $15.99

54. "MOONLIGHT IN VERMONT" AND OTHER GREAT STANDARDS
00843050 .... $15.99

55. BENNY GOLSON
00843052 .... $15.95

56. "GEORGIA ON MY MIND" & OTHER SONGS BY HOAGY CARMICHAEL
00843056 .... $15.99

57. VINCE GUARALDI
00843057 .... $16.99

58. MORE LENNON AND MCCARTNEY
00843059 .... $16.99

59. SOUL JAZZ
00843060 .... $16.99

60. DEXTER GORDON
00843061 .... $15.95

61. MONGO SANTAMARIA
00843062 .... $15.95

62. JAZZ-ROCK FUSION
00843063 .... $16.99

63. CLASSICAL JAZZ
00843064 .... $14.95

64. TV TUNES
00843065 .... $14.95

65. SMOOTH JAZZ
00843066 .... $16.99

66. A CHARLIE BROWN CHRISTMAS		
00843067		$16.99

67. CHICK COREA
00843068 .... $15.95

68. CHARLES MINGUS
00843069 .... $16.95

69. CLASSIC JAZZ
00843071 .... $15.99

70. THE DOORS
00843072 .... $14.95

71. COLE PORTER CLASSICS
00843073 .... $14.95

72. CLASSIC JAZZ BALLADS
00843074 .... $15.99

73. JAZZ/BLUES
00843075 .... $14.95

74. BEST JAZZ CLASSICS
00843076 .... $15.99

75. PAUL DESMOND
00843077 .... $16.99

76. BROADWAY JAZZ BALLADS
00843078 .... $15.99

77. JAZZ ON BROADWAY
00843079 .... $15.99

78. STEELY DAN
00843070 .... $15.99

79. MILES DAVIS CLASSICS
00843081 .... $15.99

80. JIMI HENDRIX
00843083 .... $16.99

81. FRANK SINATRA – CLASSICS
00843084 .... $15.99

82. FRANK SINATRA – STANDARDS
00843085 .... $16.99

83. ANDREW LLOYD WEBBER
00843104 .... $14.95

84. BOSSA NOVA CLASSICS
00843105 .... $14.95

85. MOTOWN HITS
00843109 .... $14.95

86. BENNY GOODMAN
00843110 .... $15.99

87. DIXIELAND
00843111 .... $16.99

88. DUKE ELLINGTON FAVORITES
00843112 .... $14.95

89. IRVING BERLIN FAVORITES
00843113 .... $14.95

90. THELONIOUS MONK CLASSICS
00841262 .... $16.99

91. THELONIOUS MONK FAVORITES
00841263 .... $16.99

92. LEONARD BERNSTEIN
00450134 .... $15.99

93. DISNEY FAVORITES
00843142 .... $14.99

94. RAY
00843143 .... $14.99

95. JAZZ AT THE LOUNGE
00843144 .... $14.99

96. LATIN JAZZ STANDARDS
00843145 .... $15.99

97. MAYBE I'M AMAZED*
00843148 .... $15.99

98. DAVE FRISHBERG
00843149 .... $15.99

99. SWINGING STANDARDS
00843150 .... $14.99

100. LOUIS ARMSTRONG
00740423 .... $16.99

101. BUD POWELL
00843152 .... $14.99

102. JAZZ POP
00843153 .... $15.99

**103. ON GREEN DOLPHIN STREET
& OTHER JAZZ CLASSICS**
00843154 .... $14.99

104. ELTON JOHN
00843155 .... $14.99

105. SOULFUL JAZZ
00843151 .... $15.99

106. SLO' JAZZ
00843117 .... $14.99

107. MOTOWN CLASSICS
00843116 .... $14.99

108. JAZZ WALTZ
00843159 .... $15.99

109. OSCAR PETERSON
00843160 .... $16.99

110. JUST STANDARDS
00843161 .... $15.99

111. COOL CHRISTMAS
00843162 .... $15.99

112. PAQUITO D'RIVERA – LATIN JAZZ*
48020662 .... $16.99

113. PAQUITO D'RIVERA – BRAZILIAN JAZZ*
48020663 .... $19.99

114. MODERN JAZZ QUARTET FAVORITES
00843163 .... $15.99

115. THE SOUND OF MUSIC
00843164 .... $15.99

116. JACO PASTORIUS
00843165 .... $15.99

117. ANTONIO CARLOS JOBIM – MORE HITS
00843166 .... $15.99

118. BIG JAZZ STANDARDS COLLECTION
00843167 .... $27.50

119. JELLY ROLL MORTON
00843168 .... $15.99

120. J.S. BACH
00843169 .... $15.99

121. DJANGO REINHARDT
00843170 .... $15.99

122. PAUL SIMON
00843182 .... $16.99

123. BACHARACH & DAVID
00843185 .... $15.99

124. JAZZ-ROCK HORN HITS
00843186 .... $15.99

126. COUNT BASIE CLASSICS
00843157 .... $15.99

127. CHUCK MANGIONE
00843188 .... $15.99

128. VOCAL STANDARDS (LOW VOICE)
00843189 .... $15.99

129. VOCAL STANDARDS (HIGH VOICE)
00843190 .... $15.99

130. VOCAL JAZZ (LOW VOICE)
00843191 .... $15.99

131. VOCAL JAZZ (HIGH VOICE)
00843192 .... $15.99

132. STAN GETZ ESSENTIALS
00843193 .... $15.99

133. STAN GETZ FAVORITES
00843194 .... $15.99

134. NURSERY RHYMES*
00843196 .... $17.99

135. JEFF BECK
00843197 .... $15.99

136. NAT ADDERLEY
00843198 .... $15.99

137. WES MONTGOMERY
00843199 .... $15.99

138. FREDDIE HUBBARD
00843200 .... $15.99

139. JULIAN "CANNONBALL" ADDERLEY
00843201 .... $15.99

140. JOE ZAWINUL
00843202 .... $15.99

141. BILL EVANS STANDARDS
00843156 .... $15.99

142. CHARLIE PARKER GEMS
00843222 .... $15.99

143. JUST THE BLUES
00843223 .... $15.99

144. LEE MORGAN
00843229 .... $15.99

145. COUNTRY STANDARDS
00843230 .... $15.99

146. RAMSEY LEWIS
00843231 .... $15.99

147. SAMBA
00843232 .... $15.99

150. JAZZ IMPROV BASICS
00843195 .... $19.99

151. MODERN JAZZ QUARTET CLASSICS
00843209 .... $15.99

152. J.J. JOHNSON
00843210 .... $15.99

154. HENRY MANCINI
00843213 .... $14.99

155. SMOOTH JAZZ CLASSICS
00843215 .... $15.99

156. THELONIOUS MONK – EARLY GEMS
00843216 .... $15.99

157. HYMNS
00843217 .... $15.99

158. JAZZ COVERS ROCK
00843219 .... $15.99

159. MOZART
00843220 .... $15.99

160. GEORGE SHEARING
14041531 .... $16.99

161. DAVE BRUBECK
14041556 .... $16.99

162. BIG CHRISTMAS COLLECTION
00843221 .... $24.99

164. HERB ALPERT
14041775 .... $16.99

165. GEORGE BENSON
00843240 .... $16.99

168. TADD DAMERON
00103663 .... $15.99

169. BEST JAZZ STANDARDS
00109249 .... $19.99

*These CDs do not include split tracks.

0413